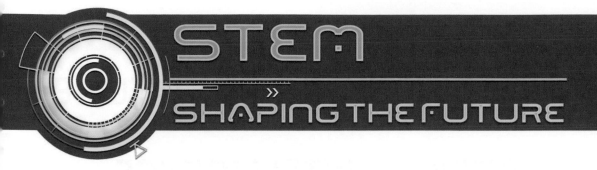

COMPUTING AND THE INTERNET

STEM: SHAPING THE FUTURE

ARTIFICIAL INTELLIGENCE

COMPUTING AND THE INTERNET

GENETIC ENGINEERING

MEDICAL DISCOVERIES

STEM
SHAPING THE FUTURE

COMPUTING AND THE INTERNET

BEATRICE KAVANAUGH

MASON CREST

Mason Crest
450 Parkway Drive, Suite D
Broomall, Pennsylvania 19008
(866) MCP-BOOK (toll free)

3 5 7 9 8 6 4 2

on file at the Library of Congress
ISBN: 978-1-4222-3710-6 (series)
ISBN: 978-1-4222-3712-0 (hc)
ISBN: 978-1-4222-8074-4 (ebook)

QR CODES AND LINKS TO THIRD-PARTY CONTENT

TABLE OF CONTENTS

KEY ICONS TO LOOK FOR:

 Words to understand: These words with their easy-to-understand definitions will increase the reader's understanding of the text while building vocabulary skills.

 Sidebars: This boxed material within the main text allows readers to build knowledge, gain insights, explore possibilities, and broaden their perspectives by weaving together additional information to provide realistic and holistic perspectives.

 Educational Videos: Readers can view videos by scanning our QR codes, providing them with additional educational content to supplement the text. Examples include news coverage, moments in history, speeches, iconic sports moments and much more!

 Text-dependent questions: These questions send the reader back to the text for more careful attention to the evidence presented there.

 Research projects: Readers are pointed toward areas of further inquiry connected to each chapter. Suggestions are provided for projects that encourage deeper research and analysis.

 Series glossary of key terms: This back-of-the book glossary contains terminology used throughout this series. Words found here increase the reader's ability to read and comprehend higher-level books and articles in this field.

WORDS TO UNDERSTAND

analog—of or relating to a device or process in which data is represented by physical quantities that change continuously; non-digital

cloud computing—the practice of storing regularly used computer data on multiple servers that can be accessed through the Internet

digital—of, relating to, or characterized by computerized technology to process data in discrete units or especially binary (zero or one) numbers

Digital Age—the modern age in which information has become a commodity that is quickly and widely disseminated and easily available, especially through the use of computer technology—also called Information Age

Digital Revolution—the advancement of technology, beginning in the late 1970s, from analog electronic and mechanical devices to digital technology

Internet—an electronic communications network that connects computer networks and organizational computer facilities around the world

smartphone—a mobile telephone that includes software functions such as sending or receiving e-mail, connecting to the Internet, taking photographs, etc.

World Wide Web (web)—a part of the Internet accessed through a graphical user interface (interactive computer screen) and containing documents often connected by hyperlinks

CHAPTER 1

HISTORY OF THE DIGITAL REVOLUTION

IN 1986, ONLY ONE PERCENT of the world's information was stored *digitally*—using computer technology to process data in numbers or discrete units—including CDs, DVDs, and computer hard drives. The other 99 percent was stored in *analog* (non-digital) form such as books, newspapers, and videotapes. By 2014, that ratio flipped upside down, with 99 percent of information in the world stored digitally and just 1 percent in analog form. Similarly, in 1986, 41 percent of the world's data-processing power was in pocket calculators and only 33 percent in personal computers. By 2007, 66 percent of processing power was in computers, and calculators did not even account for 1 percent.

These vast changes are representative of the *Digital Revolution*—the advancement of technology from analog electronic and mechanical devices to digital technology. The Digital Revolution started in the 1970s and continues today. It marked the beginning of the *Digital Age*, or Information Age, in which information has become a commodity that is quickly and widely spread and easily available, especially through the use of computer technology.

BOOK OVERVIEW

Living in the Digital Age, you probably use the Internet quite a lot, perhaps every day. But do you ever pause to think about how it is changing people's lives or even impacting those who do not have access to it? The Internet is one of many digital technologies—such as *smartphones*, cloud computing, and artificial intelligence—that

> Computers have been around since the mid-twentieth century. The first computers were big and slow, and very few people used them.

is rapidly advancing, and it is difficult to predict how these changes will affect society.

In this book, we will look at the role digital technologies play in our lives and think about some of the questions that are raised by their development. We must consider complicated but important issues that do not necessarily have a "right" or "wrong" answer—for example, if there should be limits on what the Internet can be used for, whether smartphones are helpful or harmful to people's relationships, and how those without digital devices are affected in this era.

This book will not tell you what to think or which side of an argument you should be on. It will give you historical and technical background, expose you to current trends, and ask questions that will challenge you. Then you can form your own opinions, discuss topics with others, and be able to explain and defend your points of view.

FROM THE INDUSTRIAL TO DIGITAL REVOLUTION

The Industrial Revolution of the nineteenth-century was marked by a transition from hand-production methods to machine production, water and steam power, and the factory system. This led to enormous increases in available goods, services, global population—especially in cities—and rapid growth in technology and economies around the world. Productivity improved, and the more technology advanced, the less need there

was for expensive human labor. In contrast to the mass production of goods that came from the Industrial Revolution, the Digital Revolution brought the ability to transfer information instantly by shifting from mechanical and analog technologies to digital electronics.

The origins of the Digital Age can be traced back to the work of Claude Shannon, a mathematician from the United States who published a landmark paper in 1948 proposing that information can be quantitatively encoded as a series of ones and zeroes. He demonstrated that through this system, all information in media—including telephone, radio, and television signals—could be flawlessly

Digital information is stored in what is called "binary code," consisting of the digits 0 or 1. Sequences of these digits (known as strings) can tell the computer or other electronic device to present a letter, color, or other piece of information in a certain place on the screen.

The development of transistors in the 1950s enabled electronic devices such as computers and televisions to be made smaller, while simultaneously becoming faster and more powerful.

transmitted. He became known as the "father of information theory," and his ideas would eventually lead to the advent of personal computers and the Digital Age.

In 1947, the transistor was invented at Bell Labs in the United States. This device controls the flow of electricity in electronic equipment, enabling the amplification or switching of electronic signals. When a transistor turns on or off, an electric current flows or stops accordingly—today's transistors can turn on or off 300 billion times per second. Transistors are now a key component of all microchips. Their development led to the invention of the first fully electronic and programmable computer in 1953, the transistor radio in 1954, and a transistor television (TV) in 1960. By the 1970s, personal computers and video game consoles were introduced, and analog records were starting to be converted to digital form.

ANALOG TO DIGITAL MEDIA

A major landmark in the Digital Revolution was the transition from analog to digitally recorded music during the 1980s, when the digital format of compact discs (CDs) replaced analog storage formats such as vinyl records and cassette tapes. By the end of the decade, manufacturers such as

During the 1980s, the digital format CD began to replace vinyl records as the preferred storage format for popular music. CDs had the advantage of being smaller and providing better sound quality.

> *The Commodore 64 was the best-selling personal computer of the 1980s. It was inexpensive, could be connected to a television set, and could be used to run a variety of useful programs using simple computer languages like BASIC.*

Commodore, Apple, and Tandy had made the personal computer commonplace. Motorola sold the first analog cell phone in 1983. The first digital cell phone was produced in 1991. Digital video discs (DVDs) that could hold an entire movie were introduced in 1995, and soon began to replace videotape as the preferred format for home viewing.

In the US military, sophisticated spy satellites with high-resolution cameras took pictures of enemy forces, but canisters of undeveloped film had to be retrieved in a complicated mid-air transfer that resulted in many lost photos. The "Kennan" satellite of 1976 was developed with a revolutionary electro-optical camera that transmitted images in digital format. This technology would evolve by 1988 into the digital camera.

THE INTERNET

In 1969, the Advanced Research Projects Agency Network (ARPANET) linked military computers to one another in a network that was able to share information between the Pentagon, Strategic Air Command, and bombproof defense command centers under mountain ranges. The research, protocols, and basic hardware were later made available to colleges in the US, where they were refined into what would eventually become the *Internet*—an electronic communications network that connects computers around the world.

The Internet was made available to unrestricted commercial use in 1991, and by 1993, the *World Wide Web (web)*—a set of linked pages called websites that can be

Most people access the Internet through the World Wide Web, a network of hyperlinked "pages" that contain information. The Internet and the World Wide Web have had a profound effect on the global society over the past three decades.

accessed with site addresses or hyperlinks on the Internet—was being used by corporations to create home pages where they could place text and graphics to sell products. Soon, a person could purchase anything, including airline tickets, cars, and DVDs by going online—connecting to the Internet—and browsing websites from their home computer. College students and professors alike could use the Internet to conduct research. Electronic mail, or e-mail, accessed the Internet to send and receive messages, connecting people from around the world and vastly increasing the rate of commerce.

One early problem faced by Internet users was speed because phone lines could only transmit a limited amount of information at a time. The development of fiber-optic cables allowed for mass amounts of information to be sent every second. Companies like Intel also developed faster microprocessors, so personal computers could process the incoming signals at a more rapid rate. This enabled cable television to go digital, expanding the number of channels available to customers. By 1999, almost every country had an online connection, and more than half of the US population used the Internet on a regular basis.

THE DIGITAL WORLD IN THE PALM OF YOUR HAND

In the 2000s, digital technology spread from the developed to the developing world and from the home to wherever an individual happened to be. As the Digital Revolution spread, mobile phones became more common than landline phones, the number of Internet users continued to grow, and TV started to transition from analog to digital signals. Text messaging grew into a common form of communication, and high-definition television (HDTV) became a standard broadcasting format in many countries.

The first smartphone—a mobile phone with the operating system of a personal computer and ability to connect to the Internet—was developed in Japan in 1999 but gained popularity in the US in the 2000s with phones such as the T-Mobile Sidekick and Blackberry devices. The iPhone hit the market in 2007, commercializing touchscreens and apps on mobile devices.

Social networking through the Internet became a global phenomenon in the 2000s with Friendster in 2002, LinkedIn and MySpace in 2003, and Facebook in 2004. While Friendster and MySpace are no longer commercial social networking sites, there are 433 million LinkedIn users who connect for mostly business purposes and 1.7 billion Facebook users worldwide—a startling 23 percent of the world's population.

By 2010, the Internet was accessible to more than 25 percent of the global population, and 70 percent of the world owned a mobile phone. Websites and Internet resources were integrally connected with mobile gadgets. Tablet computers such as the Apple iPad or Samsung Galaxy became wildly popular, and cloud computing—storing computer data on multiple servers that can be accessed through the Internet—allowed devices to connect to vast amounts of data and software from anywhere in the world without a large hard drive.

ECONOMICS AND SOCIAL LIFE

The digitization of information has had a profound impact on traditional media businesses, such as book publishing, the music industry, and major TV and cable networks. As information is increasingly transmitted in digital form, businesses across many industries have sharpened their focus on how to capitalize on the Digital Age.

Facebook is an online social networking service founded in February 2004 by Mark Zuckerberg and his college roommates. Today, it is one of the most valuable companies in the world.

As much as economies have been affected in this era of digital information, social relationships may have changed even more. Gone are the days of mainly communicating face-to-face or through letters or phone calls from one home to another. With social media, text messaging, and video chatting, the means of communication—and thus, relationships—are fundamentally different.

ISSUES IN THE DIGITAL AGE

With this degree of change, there are many issues that are important to consider as citizens who live in a digital world. In this country, Internet access is legally available to

A man accesses a computer at an Internet terminal in the airport in Singapore.

everyone, and you can go online from wherever you are with the right device, but the Internet and digital technology hold dangers that could threaten you directly. There are also global issues that involve you—how digitization affects people in other parts of the world has an impact on you, as it shapes global politics and economics.

The Internet is used by 89 percent of the population of North America, and more than 73 percent of the population of Europe and Australia. Those percentages are much lower in the Middle East (53.7 percent), Asia (44.2 percent), and Africa (28.6 percent). Does this further the economic and power gap between these regions?

Within countries, there are groups of people who use the Internet constantly while other segments of the population may not even know what it is. If you are young, wealthy, and educated, you probably use the Internet for multiple purposes every day. If you are elderly, poor, less educated, or live in a rural area with poor communication links, you may not use it much, if at all. In what ways is it better or worse to be connected to the online world?

REGULATING DIGITAL CONTENT

In some countries, people are allowed to say what they think, however much it may hurt or upset others. This is called freedom of speech. Freedom of information, shared digitally, is also highly valued in many places. The law gives people a right to know what is going on, even if sharing the information may have damaging results. In other countries, content may be much more restricted—but keeping people in the dark can also be damaging.

Should we be allowed to say things that are hurtful to others? Is our right to do what we want greater than someone else's right to be free from being offended? How can we balance people's rights to privacy with the need for a population's personal information to keep society secure? These are some of the questions that have come up in the Digital Age, and the more informed we are, the better we can help make decisions for everyone's benefit.

We all have a right to be involved in choices about the world's future. But in order to have the power to change things, we need to understand the issues that affect us all. You must be able to separate fact from opinion and reliable information from media hype. If you can do this and develop your own informed views, you will be able to play an important part in the Digital Age.

TEXT-DEPENDENT QUESTIONS

1. What is the difference between the Internet and the web?

2. Describe four key developments during the Digital Revolution.

3. Name two social networking sites that thrived and two that failed.

 # EDUCATIONAL VIDEO

Scan here to watch a video on Digital Revolution.

RESEARCH PROJECT

Using the Internet or your school library, research the topic of transistors, and answer the following question: "Was the transistor the greatest invention of the 20th century?"

Some say the transistor was the greatest invention because it is the key to the entire Digital Age. Without it, we would not have the radio, TV, personal computer, smart phone, or many other products we use today. No other innovation in the 20th century can claim to be the foundation for an entire new age.

Others contend that there are other inventions that were more important in the 20th century, such as the car, assembly line, or even antibiotics. Without transportation, productivity, or health advances, we would be in much worse shape as a society.

Write a two-page report, using data you have found in your research to support your conclusion, and present it to your class.

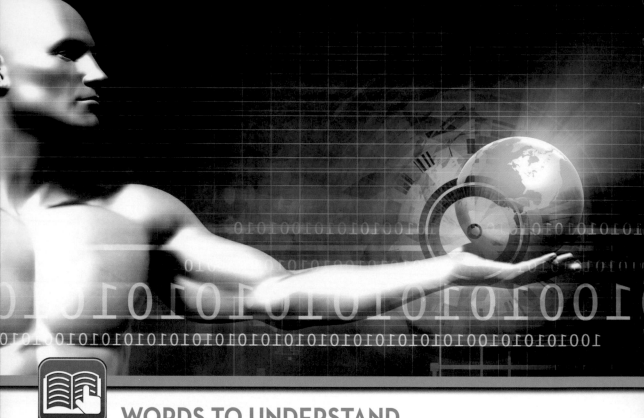

WORDS TO UNDERSTAND

android—a mobile robot usually with a human form

artificial intelligence (AI)—a branch of computer science dealing with the simulation of intelligent behavior in computers

big data—an accumulation of data that is too large and complex for processing by traditional database management tools

cyborg—a person whose body contains mechanical or electrical devices

Moore's law—a principle of microprocessor development holding that processing power doubles about every 18 months, especially relative to cost or size

personal-digital assistant (PDA)—a small handheld device equipped with a microprocessor that is used especially for storing and organizing personal information (as addresses and schedules)

prosthesis—an artificial device that replaces a missing or injured part of the body

CHAPTER 2

CURRENT ADVANCES IN DIGITAL TECHNOLOGY

FOR YOUNGER GENERATIONS, it may be difficult to imagine life without current digital applications. They may ask their elders how they kept in touch with friends and business contacts without e-mail and social networking. How did they reach a destination without Global Positioning System (GPS) technology on their cell phones? Did they really have to sit at a desk to use their computers before laptops or tablets were invented? *Moore's law* states that computer-processing power doubles every 18 months, and indeed, technology has developed at such a pace during the Digital Age. What are the latest devices, and how did they come about? What can we anticipate next?

THE RISE OF THE SMARTPHONE

The first concepts that eventually led to the invention of the smartphone date back to the 1970s, when Theodore Paraskevakos conceived of intelligence, data processing, and visual display screens in telephones. However, it was not until 1992 that IBM created the Simon Personal Communicator, a prototype mobile phone that incorporated features of a *personal-digital assistant (PDA)*—a handheld device with a microprocessor that can store and organize personal information such as addresses and schedules. On top of PDA functions, Simon could also make phone calls and send and receive e-mail and faxes.

Hand-held tablet computers and most mobile phones can be used for email and web browsing—meaning that today, people can carry their web connection in their pockets.

In 1996, Nokia released the 9000 Communicator, a cell phone with a full QWERTY keyboard and an Intel computer chip. It possessed the same abilities as Simon but added web browsing, word processing, and spreadsheets. The term "smartphone" would be coined the following year, when Ericsson released the GS 88, otherwise known as Penelope. Other companies produced similar models, but smartphones were still largely uncommon in the mass consumer market through the 1990s.

In the early 2000s, Symbian, BlackBerry, Palm, and Windows Mobile became increasingly popular brands of smartphones, but their devices were marketed mainly towards business users needing to stay connected on the go. The growing volume of these devices and the convenience of Internet from anywhere attracted the consumer market in the mid-2000s. From 2004 to 2007, there was a dramatic rise in smartphone usage, now among everyday consumers as well as business people.

THE iPHONE EFFECT

To this point, smartphones outside of the business world were primarily used for correspondence and light web browsing. This changed dramatically in 2007 when Apple CEO Steve Jobs introduced the iPhone. Apple's take on the smartphone included powerful multimedia functions, a large color display, and a digitized touch screen.

One game-changing feature of the iPhone was how websites were displayed. With a new

Apple Computer released the first iPhone in 2007. These devices, which have the power of a small computer, changed the smartphone market and inspired a variety of imitators.

"Apps" are software programs that can be downloaded to a mobile device, such as a smartphone or tablet. They can be used to connect to social-media sites like Facebook or Instagram; to send and receive email; or for a variety of other useful tasks.

web browser in Apple's operating system (iOS), web pages were no longer cumbersome versions of websites with multiple menus to scroll through but fully rendered web pages on a mobile device. The other pivotal innovation was the Apple Application (App) Store, from which users could download—or develop—a myriad of applications, including those for news, social media, shopping, music, and games.

Google answered iOS with its own mobile operating system, Android OS. Both iOS and Android dominated the operating system market for smartphones, slowly weeding out the competition. Smartphones with physical keyboards also declined over a few years as touchscreens became standard. Today, manufacturers aim to improve the capabilities of smartphones, so they can be a full camera, web browser, music player, and gaming system in addition to a phone. Features such as speaker quality, battery life, screen resolution, design, and storage space are constantly improving. The iPhone—and subsequently, all smartphones—spread throughout the non-business consumer market and essentially became a multimedia computer in the palm of one's hand.

Data from the Pew Research Center show that in 2013, less-advanced countries had a 21 percent rate of smartphone ownership, but this figure climbed to 37 percent in 2015. Developed nations had a 68 percent rate of smartphone ownership in 2015—a digital divide of 31 percentage points that is shrinking every year. And large majorities in almost every nation surveyed report owning some form of mobile device, even if they are not considered smartphones. The smartphone has become a mobile resource that connects the world to the Internet as well as each other.

DIGITAL ACCESSORIES

With Moore's law in effect, digital devices are becoming increasingly more powerful and compact. The smartphone market is now being decentralized through digital accessories and wearables that tout similar capabilities.

The Apple Watch became available to consumers in 2015, pairing with an iPhone to receive text messages, phone calls, and notifications. It also integrates with iOS and Apple applications, bringing features like fitness and health tracking to a person's wrist. Similar to the Apple Watch but focused exclusively on health, the FitBit was introduced in 2008 by founders James Park and Eric Friedman as a watch with a tracker designed to improve overall health by monitoring physical activity, diet, and sleep.

Google Glass, which arrived in 2014, is a set of glasses that displays information to the user in its lenses. Wearers communicate with the Internet through voice commands. It incorporates a touchpad on the side to swipe for viewing current events, weather, photos, social media updates, and making phone calls. It also has photo and video-recording capabilities along with applications like Google Maps, Gmail, and others made by third-party developers.

A man wears the Google Glass device, a headset with a small screen so that wearers could be constantly connected to their email or check news, weather, and social media.

Though conceived of decades earlier, computer scientist Jaron Lanier coined the term "virtual reality" (VR) in 1987. VR devices, typically headsets, immerse users in three-dimensional worlds, allowing them to see an interactive, moving environment while creating the illusion that they are in another place. VR gained popularity in the 1990s, with the chief initial use in gaming, but has also been used in military training, including battlefield, flight, and vehicle simulation. It is expected to expand to movies that will pull viewers into the environment of a film. VR-device sales are projected to reach 14 million units worldwide in 2016.

Digital technology has recently become integrated with apparel. CuteCircuit has several projects available now or in production, including the Kinetic Dress, which lights up according to the wearer's movement; the Hug Shirt that recreates the sensation of a hug—with touch and warmth—when a distant user sends a "hug" through a Bluetooth device; the M Dress which accepts a SIM card to make and receive phone calls from the dress itself; and the T-shirt-OS that can play music, take pictures, and show images and texts on the clothing.

FROM PERSONAL COMPUTERS TO TABLETS

With increasing value placed in mobility and ease of access, the tablet computer has carved out its own niche in the marketplace. In 1972, Alan Kay published a paper about the Dynabook, an all-in-one computing device incorporating advances in flat-panel display technology, user interfaces, miniaturization of computer components, and some experimental work in Wi-Fi technology. This vision became reality in the late 1980s with the Linus Write-Top and GridPad, which had flat touchscreens and a stylus to write with. Apple's MessagePad in 1993 and the PalmPilot of 1997 were the first PDAs that were in between a cell phone and laptop computer.

Microsoft and Windows developed color tablets with more functions in the 2000s, but the tablet became a widespread commercial product in 2010 with Apple's iPad, boasting a touchscreen, camera, music playability, and most apps that had been developed for the iPhone. Competitors such as Samsung created the Galaxy, while Amazon made the Kindle with an emphasis on reading at an affordable price. Today, there are laptop computers that convert to tablets as well as desktops that have touchscreens like tablets. Overall sales in 2015 for tablets declined in 2015, however, perhaps due to advances in cell phones that have larger screens and can do many of the same functions.

CLOUD COMPUTING

Cloud computing, or "the cloud," is the delivery of on-demand computing resources over the Internet on a pay-for-use basis. It relies on sharing computing resources rather than having local servers or personal devices to handle applications. In this Internet-based computing, different services—such as servers, storage, and applications—are delivered

Powerful tablets have begun to replace laptop or desktop computers, as well as textbooks, in many American classrooms.

to your computer or device through the Internet, so you do not need to have a large-capacity hard drive on your computer to store data or purchase applications that you may only need for a short time.

In a sense, the cloud allows you to "rent" storage space and software programs from a global network of resources rather than having to permanently buy them at a higher cost. Cloud-based applications—or software as a service (Saas)—run on distant computers "in the cloud" that are owned and operated by others, connecting to users' computers, usually through a web browser.

The goal of cloud computing is to enable high-performance computing power, normally used by only military and research facilities, to perform tens of trillions of computations per second in consumer-oriented applications such as financial portfolios, massive data storage, or large, immersive online computer games. To do this, cloud computing uses networks of large groups of servers to spread data-processing tasks across them.

The benefits of cloud computing include resources that can scale up or down quickly to meet specific demands, self-service access to all the Internet resources you need, and payment for only what you use. For businesses, this technology provides increased storage, flexibility, and cost reduction, but concerns exist about the security of personal or corporate data in the cloud.

BIG DATA

A human brain automatically categorizes things, but it needs see many examples before it can distinguish between cats and dogs or Indian and Korean food. The same principle holds true for computer programs. Even the most advanced computer has to play at least a thousand games of chess before it becomes a formidable opponent. An important part of current digital breakthroughs lie in the massive amount of collected data about our world, called *big data*, which provides the information that programs need to learn in any forum. Huge databases, web cookies, online footprints, years and years of search results, and the entire digital universe are at the disposal of computer programs to draw from.

If you search for a necklace online, the websites you visit after that may show advertisements for necklaces. That is big data at work, learning what types of products you are interested in, and indeed, one of the key applications of big data is understanding and targeting customers. A Google search is empowered by big data to suggest likely possibilities of what you may be looking for as you type. A computer opponent in a game will incorporate all the information from previous games to make wiser decisions. Voice recognition now has the accuracy it does because of the millions of speaking examples programs have learned from.

Big data is used by the government to analyze patterns in traffic, law enforcement, and public health to improve efficiency. With programs that can now track and organize enormous amounts of data, digital technologies can be used for a wide variety of purposes, including the development of *artificial intelligence (AI)*, the branch of computer science dealing with the simulation of intelligent behavior in computers.

HISTORY OF ARTIFICIAL INTELLIGENCE

The goal of AI research is to create machines that are "intelligent"—that can think for themselves, communicate, and act in some of the same ways as humans. Truly intelligent machines that think as independently, broadly, and creatively as humans do not yet exist, but scientists are working to develop the next generation of AI computers with a great deal of money invested in research. Perhaps it would be considered the pinnacle of the Digital Age if machines were produced that could think like humans, except with infinite data-processing abilities.

AI is a concept that dates all the way back to ancient times. Jewish legends of the golem conceived of an automated servant that was made from clay and could be brought to life by placing a magic token in its mouth. Removing the token would return the golem to unanimated clay. The idea of intelligent robots was also found in the Greek myths of Hephaestus—a blacksmith who manufactured mechanical servants—and the bronze man, Talos.

Modern history in AI begins with the stored-program computer, invented by John von Neumann in 1953. In 1956, John McCarthy coined the term "artificial intelligence" at the Dartmouth Conference. The same year, Allen Newell, J.C. Shaw, and Herbert Simon developed the first AI computer program, the Logic Theorist.

In 1997, IBM's Deep Blue became the first

Amazing improvements in artificial intelligence were shown in 2011, when the IBM Watson computer defeated two former champions, Ken Jennings and Brad Rutter, on the television show *Jeopardy*.

computer to defeat a chess champion when it won against grandmaster Gary Kasparov. In 2005 and 2007, respectively, robots drove 131 miles on a new desert trail and successfully navigated 55 miles of an urban environment while following traffic laws. The answering system Watson won the quiz show *Jeopardy* in 2011 against former champions Brad Rutter and Ken Jennings. In 2014, Eugene Goostman developed a chatbot, a computer program that simulates human conversation with people over the Internet. It convinced one-third of test judges that it was a human being responding in dialogue, though this was partly due to its claim that it was an adolescent that spoke English as a second language.

In the past, machines replaced people in repetitive, unskilled tasks such as factory work. However, as AI becomes more sophisticated, it is increasingly able to take on skilled labor and aid in complex work. In the workforce, education, military, and even childcare, AI is showing the potential to be a valuable asset to society.

ANDROIDS AND CYBORGS

It is fairly easy to think of robots as machines as long as they remain visually mechanical. But if we make robots that have a skin-like covering, fur, or other animal attributes—we may find it harder to recognize them as machines. Work is underway not only to build *androids*—robots that look like humans—but also to make a reality of *cyborgs*—humans

SIDEBAR

CYBORG PROFESSOR

Kevin Warwick, Professor of Cybernetics at the University of Reading, is a cyborg—part human, part machine. He has had small electronic devices fitted into his body and connected to his nervous system. The first implant allowed him to be tracked around a building, as well as have doors open and lights turned on as he approached. The second linked his nervous system to the Internet, and the third enabled him to control a robot arm on the other side of the Atlantic Ocean. He hopes to eventually be able to download his feelings and thoughts and store them in a computer. He also aims to communicate directly with other people with similar devices—his wife now has an implant as well in order to help him experiment.

whose bodies contain mechanical or electrical devices—by giving real people and animals robotic functions.

Studies have shown we respond better to robots that have human characteristics, including skin, hair, and body movements. In 2013, scientists at Georgia Tech University developed a robotic skin with thousands of tiny, mechanical hairs that generate electricity when brushed or exposed to pressure. This allows a robot wearing the skin to have a sense of "touch," which could be eventually used in *prostheses*—artificial devices that replace a missing or injured part of the body—or in returning sensation to people who have lost limbs.

In 2016, researchers at the Tokyo Institute of Technology created a robot with a human skeleton and microfilament "muscle" tissues that connect to joints and contract and expand like human muscles. In fact, the robot has the same number of muscles in its leg as people do and can execute smooth movements. However, it is still lacking in strength and needs assistance to walk.

NADINE AND SOPHIA

Combining multiple technologies, robots resembling and interacting like humans have now been developed. Nadine is an android made in 2013 by the Nanyang Technological University in Singapore. With soft skin and flowing brunette hair, Nadine resembles her creator, Professor Nadia Thalmann, as she performs work as a university receptionist. Not only does she greet visitors, smile, make eye contact, and shake hands, but she can even recognize past guests and start conversations based on previous chats. She has her own "personality," expressing happiness or sadness based on the topic of conversation. Her AI is based on technology similar to Apple's Siri and Microsoft's Cortana, and Thalmann says social robots can address needs for child care, socialization with the elderly, and even health-care services in future.

In 2015, Dr. David Hanson of Hanson Robotics created Sophia, an android with lifelike silicon skin that can emulate more than 62 facial

Professor Nadia Magnenat Thalmann has pioneered research into virtual humans for more than 30 years. Her android Nadine has been called the "World's most human-like robot."

expressions. With cameras inside her "eyes" combined with computer algorithms, she is able to "see," follow faces, make eye contact, and recognize individuals. Using tools like Alphabet's Google Chrome voice-recognition technology, Sophia can understand speech, speak on topic, and learn over time. Hanson said that he believes one day, robots will be indistinguishable from humans, with the ability to walk, play, teach, help, and form real relationships with people. With aging populations and a reduced workforce in many countries, androids like Nadine and Sophia may help to meet practical needs in communities around the world. In other areas, they may replace human employees and force a shift in the labor market.

AI IN THE WORKFORCE

AI systems are already at work in factories—automating many unskilled labor processes— but as expert computer systems in areas such as law and medicine improve, they might take over some parts of skilled human jobs as well. A doctor or lawyer may no longer need such detailed knowledge if they could call on an AI program to support their judgements or diagnoses.

Creativity is another area of possibilities for AI. It is already possible to get hold of very basic story-writing programs, and computers can put together simple bits of music. An AI system could try out its compositions on people to see which they like and analyze big data in popular music or literature written by people. If it followed trends and learned from ongoing human feedback, it could eventually create popular new entertainment.

AI is already being used effectively in education. Imagine a teacher who knows everything, has superb teaching skills, uses many different approaches to learning to suit your needs—and never gets tired of explaining the same idea in different ways. "Jill Watson," a virtual teaching assistant (TA) based on IBM's Watson platform, acted as one of nine TAs in an online course at Georgia Institute of Technology in 2016. She helped answer many of the 10,000 questions from 300 students in online forums, and none of the students knew they were interacting with an AI program, as she was answering questions with 97 percent certainty. As technology advances, will an AI device be able to assist in a live classroom? What about important teacher qualities such as enthusiasm, care for student progress, and a sense of humor?

In medicine, AI is already being used for diagnosis and treatment. In 2015, IBM acquired Merge Healthcare, which helps doctors store and access medical images. With 30 billion images to "train" its Watson software, IBM is hoping to create AI that can diagnose and treat ailments like cancer and heart disease. Modernizing Medicine is a program that taps into the collective knowledge of 3,700 medical providers, 14 million patient visits, and data on how doctors have treated patients with similar profiles. It can instantly mine data and offer treatment recommendations accordingly, which is how the medical community currently makes decisions. AI cannot yet replace doctors at a patient's bedside, but if it eventually can be a physical caregiver, would patients grieve the loss of human interaction or feel relieved someone is not seeing them every day in a fragile state? We would need to assess each person's needs carefully.

TEXT-DEPENDENT QUESTIONS

1. What two features of the iPhone in 2007 distinguished it from previous smartphones?

2. Name three main benefits that cloud computing provides.

3. What are two ways big data can impact individuals and two ways it can improve government efficiency?

4. What is the difference between an android and a cyborg?

5. Describe two ways AI can be used in medicine.

EDUCATIONAL VIDEO

Scan here to watch a video on big data.

RESEARCH PROJECT

Using the Internet or your school library, research the topic of big data and privacy, and answer the following question: "Should big data be collected by the government from people's personal Internet use?"

Some believe big data should not be gathered from personal Internet use because it is an invasion of privacy. The government does not have the right to know what we are buying, watching, or communicating on our personal devices. There are real people in the government who are privy to deeply personal information, and that is not right.

Others argue that although some privacy is sacrificed, it is necessary for the government to analyze private Internet use for security. Terrorist attacks that can harm or kill many people cannot be thwarted without analyzing big data. Also, with information from health and spending practices, public policies may be developed to better society as a whole.

Write a two-page report, using data you have found in your research to support your conclusion, and present it to your class.

WORDS TO UNDERSTAND

24-hour society— a modern society in which people can buy goods, work, go to restaurants, etc. all night and all day

Arab Spring—a series of antigovernment uprisings affecting Arab countries of North Africa and the Middle East beginning in 2010

bandwidth—a measurement of the ability of an electronic communications device or system (such as a computer network) to send and receive information

consumerism—an attitude that values the purchase of goods that are desirable but not essential

e-commerce—activities that relate to the buying and selling of goods and services over the Internet

exabyte—a unit of information equal to one billion gigabytes

CHAPTER 3

ECONOMIC AND SOCIAL IMPACT

THE DIGITAL AGE HAS GIVEN people around the world access to seemingly unlimited information, vast practical resources, and a global community. We are not only able to do more with digital devices on the Internet, but we can also connect from wherever we may be, 24 hours a day. Just as the Industrial Age—and its mass-produced goods and services—brought dramatic changes to society and the way people lived, so the Digital Age is doing the same with its proliferation of information. How is this era impacting the world economically? How is it changing the way we relate to one another socially? Are these influences positive or negative for people?

THE EXABYTE

So much digital data now moves around the world that we no longer use the term, "gigabyte" to describe global storage. That has been replaced by the "exabyte," one billion gigabytes, showing just how data-intensive the world has become in the Digital Age.

In 2002, digital storage capacity overtook analog storage—mostly paper and videotapes—for the first time. Some say this was the turning point of the Digital Age. By 2007, 94 percent of all information was stored digitally. That number had increased to 99 percent by 2014.

The global capacity to store digital information—on personal computers, smartphones, CDs and other digital devices—totaled 276 exabytes in 2007, equivalent to data in a stack of CDs from the top of your desk to 50,000 miles beyond the moon.

Around the world, cybercafés like this one in Chengdu, China, have made the Internet available to many people who would not otherwise own or use a computer.

Humans generate enough data—from TV and radio broadcasts, telephone conversations, and Internet traffic—to fill the 276-exabyte-storage capacity every eight weeks, but most of the digital traffic is never stored long-term. Does this mean that much of what we use digitally is not worthwhile?

SPEED AND ACCESS

Our connections to the Internet are now faster than ever, and increased connection speeds make a huge difference to what we can do online. Before fiber-optic cables were introduced, watching video on the Internet was almost impossible because of the limited information that could be transmitted through phone lines. But now we can stream music and watch live-video feeds from mobile phones as well as desktop computers. Before the Digital Age, we had to go to a theater or rent a VHS tape to watch a film, but now we can view a Netflix movie instantly. We can use live streaming to view concerts and other events we could not otherwise get to in the real world.

Entertainment is not the only area of access we now have from our devices. We can find out information immediately on almost any topic online. We can do our shopping, book tickets, manage our money, buy and sell in online auctions, communicate with distant friends and relatives, and even work from home or while away on a trip.

Not everyone wants to use the Internet for everyday tasks. Some people object to the anonymity of the web and prefer the personal service offered by a bank, shop, or travel agent. They may feel insecure about typing their details into a computer or unsure about the product they are purchasing. Perhaps they would rather pay a bit more to get what they want than worry

The rise of the Internet has changed peoples' shopping habits. Today, consumers can purchase almost anything on the World Wide Web, no matter where they live.

about having to search for it online. Still, a rapidly increasing population is going online for resources across the globe, and this has major economic implications moving forward.

CONSUMERISM IN THE DIGITAL ECONOMY

People have always had basic needs such as food, clothing, and shelter. As societies grew wealthier and technology advanced, however, people's appetites changed. They became interested in acquiring things that they did not need for survival. *Consumerism* is an attitude that values the purchase of goods that are desirable but not essential.

In a consumerist society where there is instant access to purchasing and selling goods and services online—also known as *e-commerce*—people can become caught up in the process of shopping and take part of their identity from the new items they buy. They may be concerned with the clothes, cars, and household furnishings they purchase because these things build an image they wish to project about themselves.

Modern consumers expect a wider selection of products and services, as well as the freedom to buy them whenever they wish. As a result, the world is fast becoming a *24-hour society*, where goods and services can be purchased at any time of the day or night—from any device they may have with them at the moment. While many stores are open from 7:00 a.m. until 11:00 p.m., almost all online businesses process transactions 24 hours a day, 7 days a week. Vacations, books, food, banking, and legal services can be purchased at any time year round. This allows people to do their shopping at a time that suits them, while producers can sell nonstop. The 24-hour society has also changed the world of work, with many people working longer and more varied hours than the traditional nine-to-five workday.

THE POWER OF E-COMMERCE

Jeff Bezos founded Amazon.com in 1994 out of his garage and was earning $20,000 per week within two months by selling books. By 2015, Amazon rose to the largest Internet-based retailer in the world, selling a diverse range of products, including electronic goods, household items, multimedia downloads, streaming content, and cloud-computing services. In that year, it had 230,800 employees, 304 million active customer accounts, and net sales totaling $107.1 billion. Such is the power of e-commerce in the Digital Age.

E-commerce offers consumer advantages including searching for specific items online without having to search through aisles or call a store; easily comparing prices to find the best deals; saving time and gas money not having to drive from place to place; and often times, having goods delivered without paying shipping costs.

For producers, e-commerce means saving money not having to pay employees or rent in a brick-and-mortar store, 24-hour selling, gathering big data on consumer shopping preferences, and the expansion of a customer base from a local area to the entire world.

Amazon.com was originally founded in the mid-1990s as an online bookstore, but it has branched out and today the website sells a wide variety of products. Today, the company's annual sales exceed $100 billion.

With advantages for both consumers and producers, business is being changed by digital technology.

Products in the Digital Age have shifted to suit customer preferences for mobile products that are always accessible. The newest computers do not even have a physical drive to play CDs, DVDs, or Blu-ray discs because online entertainment has a wealth of streaming and downloading services for music and movies. As discussed, hardware and software is also being replaced by cloud services.

Related economies are booming as a result of online shopping. The McKinsey Global Report revealed that worldwide spending on Internet advertising was $109.69 billion in 2013, but rose to $127.35 billion in 2014, a 16.1 percent increase in one year. Internet advertising accounted for 28.2 percent of all advertising in the world. The shipping industry, especially in trucking, has also skyrocketed due to e-commerce. In 2012, the American Trucking Association predicted that by 2023, the number of trucks and total tonnage carried in the US will grow by 26 percent, with a 66 percent increase in overall revenue. This means more jobs for truckers—an 11 percent growth is expected between 2012 and 2022.

Everyday individuals at home have become bona fide sellers in the digital economy. With websites such as Craigslist and eBay, anyone can advertise and sell goods or services from their home. Even in transportation, companies like Uber allow people to make money as door-to-door drivers when customers order a ride online.

COSTS OF E-COMMERCE

While e-commerce is producing jobs and bigger markets in some industries, it is also making a negative impact in other industries. In a 2016 research study, Morgan Stanley analysts estimated that Amazon accounts for about 7 percent of overall US apparel sales and will reach 19 percent by 2020. By their estimates, the online giant is already selling more clothing than all US retailers but the biggest, Wal-Mart Stores, Inc. This has led to declining sales in department stores, with Macy's, Kohl's, and Nordstrom reporting sharp drops in profits in 2016.

Similarly, businesses such as bookstores and traditional travel agencies have also seen sales evaporate as customers have been empowered to do their own purchasing on the Internet. This is not exclusive to large stores, but small businesses also find it difficult to compete against wholesale prices of large online services. Even in the booming trucking sector, what will happen if self-driving AI programs remove the need for human truck

The success of online retailers has come at the cost of many local businesses, which cannot compete and must close their doors.

drivers? The decline of these businesses mean fewer jobs and a workforce that is scrambling to adapt.

Another financial drawback of digital technology is crime on the Internet, including scams where sellers take money without delivering promised goods and identity theft in which criminals purchase items for themselves with the credit card of an innocent victim. These examples of "cybercrime" has called the attention of law enforcement to address means of prevention and punishment to protect the public.

THE DIGITAL DIVIDE

In 2015, more than 40 percent of the world's population had access to the Internet. Among the poorest 20 percent of households, nearly 7 out of 10 had a mobile phone. In fact, the poorest households are more likely to have access to

Children living in a rural Malaysian village are enthralled by a video broadcast on a smartphone. Often, poor people in developing countries do not have access to computer technologies or the Internet.

cell phones than to toilets or clean water. However, countries use opportunities offered by information technologies in different ways. And those who cannot not afford an online-accessible device or a monthly access fee are denied the possibilities of cheaper products or job opportunities that are available on the web.

People who are online have access to information that can help them improve their quality of life. They can get better deals on everything from flights to bank savings, save time with online shopping, find jobs on the Internet, and communicate for free with potential employers or business partners. Those without such resources—more likely, the poor or elderly—are left further and further behind in available time and money.

Critics have charged that this technological divide has increased the gap between the "haves" and "have-nots." In 2014, the richest 1 percent held 48 percent of global wealth, and the next wealthiest 19 percent owned another 46.5 percent, leaving the remaining 80 percent of the world with just 5.5 percent of global wealth. The bottom 80 percent had an average wealth of $3,851 per adult—1/700th of the average wealth of the richest 1 percent. The world's richest 20 percent account for 76.6 percent of total private consumption. The world's poorest 20 percent consume only 1.5 percent. Is the digital divide making these statistics even worse? Should we be protecting people from getting left behind?

In 2002, those in developed countries had access to eight times the bandwidth, or information-carrying capacity, of people in poorer nations. By 2007, that gap had almost doubled. The Pew Research Center reported that in 2015, 54 percent of people across 21 developing countries reported using the internet or owning a smartphone. By comparison, a median of 87 percent use the internet in 11 advanced economies surveyed in the same year, including the U.S. and Canada, major Western European nations, developed Pacific nations—Australia, Japan, and South Korea—and Israel. This represents a 33-percentage-point gap compared with emerging and developing nations.

SOCIAL IMPACT OF THE DIGITAL AGE

On top of huge economic shifts, the way we interact with one another has been profoundly affected by digital technologies. In the Industrial Age, we could meet someone, talk to them on a landline phone, or write a letter that took days to deliver. Today, we can pick up a cell phone and use video chatting to immediately have a face-to-face digital conversation with anyone in the world.

GPS allows us to quickly navigate to someone's home or a meeting place like a coffee shop, but the proliferation of social media has made communication an increasingly digital interaction. With nearly one-quarter of the global population on Facebook—and the growing popularity of platforms such as Instagram, Twitter, and SnapChat—people are able to meet and interact without boundaries. They can view photos or videos of someone's experiences on a daily basis or follow the daily lives of their favorite celebrities.

While the scope of people's contacts and volume of interactions has increased greatly, many argue that the depth of personal relationships has gone in the opposite direction. Many decry the impersonal nature of social networking compared to a telephone call or a handwritten letter. People are able to post status updates and photos of themselves that may not be a true representation of how they are doing. Text messages cannot convey the same level of emotion, creativity, or conversation depth as a live meeting.

SIDEBAR

ELIZA THE COMPUTER THERAPIST

In 1966, a computer system called Eliza was programmed to act like a therapist. It was not an actual AI system—it merely used a simple questioning technique. Eliza responded to people's comments and questions with more questions, much as a human counselor might do to help someone get to the bottom of their problems. Eliza did not understand the clients' feedback in any meaningful sense but used keywords to trigger questions that were likely to be suitable. To the surprise of researchers, Eliza was immensely popular.

TALKING WITH AI

Not only is more of the world's communication digital, but there is also a greater amount of "social" interaction between humans and machines. When you use a cell phone, you often end up talking to a computer program of some sort. You might leave a message on voice-mail, give commands to book tickets, or navigate a menu with voice prompts. As we continue to develop intelligent systems, there may be many more situations in which people interact with machines. Maybe telephone or online help desks could use AI systems to deal with calls. Would this work?

A 2013 report by Kleiner, Perkins, Caufield, and Byers indicated that people in the US check their cell phones 150 times per day on average. On both smartphones and the Internet, there are a growing number of interactive AI programs such as Apple's Siri, the Amazon Echo, Google Now, and Microsoft's Cortana. They can verbally answer factual questions posed by a human, play requested music, provide driving directions, buy movie tickets, and even give humorous responses. Such programs make interfacing with a computer seem more like talking to a person, and it is becoming more and more difficult to tell the difference.

Some people have a hard time accepting that the characters in television soap operas are not real people. They may write to the actors, expecting them to be the characters they play. There could be similar difficulties for some people in recognizing that a voice they talk to on the phone does not belong to a real person but is in fact a computer or AI system. As AI software increasingly resembles humans, this issue will become very difficult, as it may not always be possible to tell if the "person" facing you is human at all.

DEEPER CONVERSATIONS

Many people find that talking to a trained counselor or psychotherapist helps them with their problems. This might be a task you think a machine could not possibly do, but recent trials of computerized therapy systems have often had very positive results. People seem to feel that they can keep their dignity intact and preserve their privacy if they talk to a machine instead of a person.

Every day, millions of Americans interact on social media programs like Facebook, Snapchat, Twitter, and Instagram.

We would need to decide what should happen to the information given to an AI therapy program and what should be done with any conclusions the program drew from it. There are strict rules about what a human doctor, therapist, or pastor can do with information given in confidence. We would need similar, and perhaps additional, protection for people confiding in an AI program that could be hacked into.

POLITICS ONLINE

In many countries, government information and actions are now available for the public to view online. People who use the Internet have the chance to find out more about political and social issues that affect them. Some countries are working toward online voting for elections, allowing people to vote from home and increasing voting representation for elections. At the moment, one of the barriers to voting is the need to travel to a polling station. Online voting might mean that people with Internet access would be more likely to vote than those without it, potentially changing the balance of votes cast.

The election of Barack Obama as President of the United States in 2008 and 2012 is partly attributed to successful advertising on social media sites, including voting reminders on Twitter and interactions with the public on Facebook. During his 2012 campaign, Obama had nearly 20 times as many re-tweets of his messages as his opponent, Mitt Romney. Subsequent elections at all levels of government now incorporate social networking in their campaigns.

Widespread reports from North Africa and the Middle East suggested that social media contributed to—or even prompted—political protests such as the Tunisian Revolution in 2010. This led to a wave of demonstrations, protests, and civil wars in Arab countries known as the *Arab Spring*. Cries against unjust rulers led to internal battles in Syria, Libya, and Yemen as well as uprisings in Egypt and Bahrain. Demonstrations in a host of other Arab nations ensued. Facebook and Twitter were vehicles to spread news of political crimes by governments, organize protesters, and spread awareness to the rest of the world.

For much of his 2016 presidential campaign, businessman Donald Trump did not run the sort of political advertisements that candidates typically produce for television, radio, or Internet audiences. Instead, Trump's campaign relied on social media to attract voters.

TEXT-DEPENDENT QUESTIONS

1. Name three advantages each for consumers and producers from e-commerce.

2. What are two types of crime to be careful of in the Digital Age?

3. In what ways can social media affect the depth of personal relationships?

 EDUCATIONAL VIDEO

Scan here to watch a video on social media.

RESEARCH PROJECT

Using the Internet or your school library, research the topic of e-commerce, and answer the following question: "Is e-commerce beneficial to society?"

Some claim that e-commerce is helpful because it allows the opportunity to shop, arrange transportation, and even work at any time of the day or night, providing greater flexibility, time, and convenience.

Others contend that e-commerce is not beneficial to society because it leads to people becoming increasingly materialistic and buying products they do not need. Shoppers also stay home much more, reducing the amount of physical activity and social interaction. E-commerce has led to stores closing and people losing their jobs.

Write a two-page report, using data you have found in your research to support your conclusion, and present it to your class.

WORDS TO UNDERSTAND

censor—to examine books, movies, letters, etc., in order to remove things that are considered to be offensive, immoral, harmful to society, etc.

civil liberty—the right of people to do or say things that are not illegal without being stopped or interrupted by the government

cybersecurity—measures taken to protect a computer or computer system (as on the Internet) against unauthorized access or attack

encrypt—to change (information) from one form to another especially to hide its meaning

intellectual property—property (as an idea, invention, or process) that derives from the work of the mind or intellect; also: an application, right, or registration relating to this

pirated—illegally copied without permission

ransomware—a type of malicious software designed to block access to a computer system until a sum of money is paid

CHAPTER 4

REGULATING DIGITAL CONTENT

SHOULD THE USE OF THE INTERNET be regulated, and if so, by whom? Some parts of the web are organized—the allocation of domain names (web addresses), for instance. But it is difficult to monitor all the content posted on the web because of the sheer volume, and standards may differ internationally. Some people think there should be some control, but views on what should or should not be allowed—including what we need protecting from and who needs protecting—differ widely. Maybe we all need to be shielded from pornography, or perhaps adults should be free to see this type of content. Maybe people should not be allowed to spread information that could cause unrest or violence. But what if it is for a revolution against an unjust government?

Crime and danger are unfortunately part of the Digital Age. From pirating music and movies to hacking information from people or the government, illegal activity is also advancing with technology. People send out viruses to the masses, disrupting work or shutting down devices. Illegal information, such as how to make banned drugs or carry out

A vendor sells "pirated" copies of music CDs and movie DVDs at a market in Thailand. Piracy—the theft of intellectual property, including films, books, software, and music—is rampant in Asia. A 2013 report by a US Congressional committee determined the annual cost of this theft to be hundreds of billions of dollars.

terrorist attacks, can also be shared internationally. How can we stop criminal use of digital technology while allowing everyone else to use it as they wish?

PLAYING FAIR

Not all information is intended for sharing freely. People who make a living from writing, making music or films, and other creative activities cannot afford to give away their work for free. But the Internet provides the means for people to both share and steal.

FBI ANTI-PIRACY WARNING

The unauthorized reproduction or distribution of this copyrighted work is illegal. Criminal copyright infringement, including infringement without monetary gain, is investigated by the FBI and is punishable by up to 5 years in federal prison and a fine of $250,000.

Most movies sold for home viewing will include this notice about copyright from the Federal Bureau of Investigation (FBI).

With digital technology, people can quickly move information to anywhere in the world—and anyone can make content available on the web. So it has become easy for people to distribute *pirated*, or illegal, copies of videos, music, and software online. If you know where to look, you can find current music and just-released films to download for free. These are illegal, unauthorized versions that may be distributed from stolen copies. Pirated multimedia means the creators of the original work do not get the money they ought to and is the digital equivalent of theft from a store.

Intellectual property rights are the ownership claims that an author, composer, or artist has to their work. Businesses have intellectual property rights to new inventions, documents they publish, ideas, films, and other kinds of production. The laws covering intellectual property are intended to protect people whose work is not in making physical objects but in creative thought, and violators can be charged for copyright infringement. These laws also prevent unauthorized use of pictures and written content.

You have most likely seen an FBI warning about unauthorized copying at the beginning of a DVD or Blu-ray movie. The same laws apply to music, software, and other online created content. When you purchase digital work such as software, you do not become the owner of the copyright. Rather, you are purchasing the right to use the software under certain parameters set by the copyright owner, typically the publisher.

Federal law enforces severe civil and criminal penalties for the unauthorized reproduction, distribution, rental, or digital transmission of copyrighted materials, including sound recordings and pictures. A civil lawsuit could hold you responsible for as much as $150,000 in damages per item copied. Criminal charges by the government may leave you with a felony record, up to five years of jail time, and fines up to $250,000.

FAIR USE LAW

Copyright laws in many countries allow a small portion of copyright material to be copied without permission as long as it counts as "fair use." This is not clearly defined in every situation, but fair use generally promotes freedom of expression by permitting unlicensed use of copyright-protected works in certain circumstances, including criticism, comment, news reporting, teaching, scholarship, and research. Only small parts of a copyrighted work can be copied, and they should not be used to make a profit. The source of the material should be shown clearly.

CYBERSECURITY

Businesses will pay a lot of money to get hold of someone's personal information if they think they can make a profit from it. They might, for example, want a person's contact details in order to try to sell them something. The Internet makes it very easy for people to share—and steal—information of this kind. How could this affect you? Many countries have laws that protect people from information about them being misused. In the

Wikileaks is an international non-profit organization that publishes submissions of otherwise unavailable documents from anonymous news sources and leaks. In 2016, the organization released thousands of emails that had been stolen by hackers from the Democratic Party's national committee. The email leak embarrassed party leaders and led to a renewed focus on cybersecurity.

United Kingdom (UK), for example, the Data Protection Act states that people who want to store information about others must first register with the Information Commissioner. They have to say what they are going to do with the information, agree to use it only for the purpose specified, and let any person see a copy of the information held on them. This means a school is allowed to hold information about students that is useful to them in educating and caring for them, but they are not allowed to sell student details to a company that might want to encourage them to join a film club, for example.

INTRUSIONS AND RANSOMWARE

In the US, the FBI has identified two key priorities in *cybersecurity*—measures taken to protect a personal computer or computer system on the Internet against unauthorized access or attack. The first is computer and network intrusions. Billions of dollars are lost every year repairing systems hit by such attacks that may take down vital systems, disrupting and sometimes disabling the work of hospitals, banks, and emergency services around the country.

With illegal access to digital information, businesses trying to gain an upper hand may hack competitor websites; criminals may attempt to steal your personal information and sell it on black markets; and terrorists may look to rob our nation of vital information or launch strikes through the Internet. In order to address these threats, the FBI has special agents investigating these crimes just as they do physical crimes. Agents protect against computer intrusions, theft of intellectual property and personal information, child pornography and exploitation, and online fraud.

The second major cybercrime the FBI works against is *ransomware*—malicious software (malware) that locks valuable digital files and demands a ransom to release them. Some of the entities attacked in this way are hospitals, school districts, state and local governments, law enforcement agencies, and small or large businesses.

In a ransomware attack, victims may receive an e-mail addressed to them with an attachment that appears legitimate—like an invoice or an electronic fax—but which actually contains a malicious ransomware code. Or the e-mail might contain a link to a website that infects a computer with malware. The FBI prosecutes ransomware and also promotes prevention efforts and backup plans in case ransomware affects a computer system.

NATIONAL BOUNDARIES

Laws about what can be done with personal details online vary from country to country. An organization in the US will have to follow its national rules. But if information about you is kept on a computer in another country, US laws may not protect you. Someone will have to tell you if they move your details to, say, the UK—but once they are there,

In 2016, hackers accessed computer systems belonging to both the Republican and Democratic parties, leading to fears that they could affect the outcome of the presidential election.

UK laws apply. If you type your details into a web page hosted in Poland, Polish laws apply. The European Union (EU) and the US are currently arguing about what can be done with information about people. At the moment, they allow different things. Where does that leave you? You may not know what information is held about you, where it is kept, or what people are allowed to do with it.

IDENTITY THEFT

People who break into computer systems by finding passwords, or by other means, are called hackers. Many hackers break into systems for financial gain, but others do so just to prove they can. Other hackers break in to disrupt a system or to steal information. Identity theft—increasingly facilitated by the Internet—occurs when someone illegally gains access to another's personal information and uses it to commit theft or fraud. These digital thieves seek key pieces of information such as your name, Social Security number, date of birth, health insurance number, address, passport numbers, financial account numbers, passwords, and telephone numbers to commit their crimes.

According to U.S. government statistics, identity theft cost Americans nearly $25 billion in 2012, the most recent year for which data is available. Approximately 16.6 million Americans experienced at least one identity theft incident that year.

Many people fear that hackers will break into their bank account or take their credit card details from a computer and use them to shop. Or a hacker might be hired for a revenge attack—harming someone by sending abusive e-mail in their name, for instance. Private detectives no longer just follow people and listen in to their phone calls. Now they can pay a hacker to find out all about someone by accessing their computer files and intercepting their e-mail.

The US Congress passed the Identity Theft and Assumption Deterrence Act in

SIDEBAR

E-PIRACY GUIDELINES

- You may download and stream music, movies, or software from sites authorized by the owners of the copyrighted content, whether or not such sites charge a fee.

- It is never permitted to download unauthorized material from pirate sites or peer-to-peer systems, such as torrent sites that transfer files.

- It is illegal to make unauthorized copies of your own multimedia available to others—uploading music—on peer-to-peer systems.

1998, making identity theft a federal crime. In 2004, it followed up with the Identity Theft Penalty Enhancement Act, which established penalties for "aggravated" identity theft—using the identity of another person to commit felony crimes, including immigration violations, theft of another's Social Security benefits, and acts of domestic terrorism.

SAFE SHOPPING

Even without hackers, all computer systems have some degree of vulnerability because they are operated by people—and people can make mistakes, act wrongly, misunderstand what they are meant to do, or accept money to reveal secrets. Once information is on a computer system, it could be at risk.

Some shopping and other websites encourage users to set up "one-click buying." For people who use the same computer and credit card all the time, this is a quick way of shopping. Instead of giving their credit card details every time they want to buy something, the details are stored on computer. The sites urge people to use this only in a safe place—such as at home—but even then, it is risky. If any visitor sees your one-click account details, they can use your money.

PRIVACY MATTERS

The Internet has made communicating and sharing information very easy, but it is also made it simple for others to tap into our communications, monitor our online activity, and uncover private details about us. If you use e-mail, the web, chat rooms, or make online purchases, what you do on your computer can be tracked. Those watching could be anyone from online retailers to the government. They may claim they are gathering data for your protection or improving your user experience, but it compromises your privacy.

Some software that is downloaded can provide someone else access to your whole computer database. In this way, information can be stolen without you knowing it. The information can include what software you have, which web pages you have visited, or even the content of files on your hard disk. If you install a program on your computer to play music, for instance, you may find that it often tries to access the Internet even when you do not want it to. When you play music, it may send a copy of your playlist to a database collecting information about what music people are listening to. This might sound quite harmless—but programs of this type can gather other personal details from your system to send it out.

Computer networks in schools and businesses are set up so that everyone has a personal identity—a login name and password that lets them use their personal files and accounts. These are set up and looked after by a systems administrator, who may also be able to look at your work on the computer and reset your passwords. In many organizations, especially those that do not allow computer use for personal matters, the systems administrator may be asked to check on people's computer activity—or forced to by law enforcement if there is suspicion of illegal activity.

To protect computers against being searched, some use *encryption* programs, which code data in a way that is difficult to decipher in order to keep communications private. Computer documents and e-mail can be encrypted using very powerful codes that are extremely hard to break, even using other computers.

SURVEILLANCE AND SECURITY

Every e-mail you write, every phone call you make, and every text message you send on your mobile could be scanned by the government. International surveillance systems track satellite communications around the world. Millions of calls and messages are intercepted every day, and software is used to scan each one for suspicious content.

Many people are concerned about their communications and online activity being monitored by humans who can make mistakes and leak information or use what they find for harmful purposes. They argue that it invades privacy and means that our *civil liberties*—our rights as citizens are not being protected.

Authorities argue that they need to be able to track and read communications to help in the fight against crime. Yet a person may want to keep something secret even if it is not illegal. In response

Today there are electronic surveillance cameras in many public places.

to the September 11, 2001, terrorist attacks in the US, President George W. Bush and Congress passed the USA Patriot Act, which gave new powers to the US Department of Justice, the National Security Agency (NSA), and other federal agencies the ability to conduct surveillance on domestic and international electronic communications. It also removed legal barriers that had blocked law enforcement, intelligence, and defense agencies from sharing information about potential terrorist threats and coordinating efforts to respond to them. However, there was widespread concern about rights to privacy being violated and the government abusing its powers.

Americans participate in a demonstration against government surveillance tactics outside the Capitol building in Washington, DC.

In 2003, Edward Snowden, an employee of the NSA, noticed how far reaching the NSA's everyday surveillance of US citizens went. He collected top-secret documents regarding its domestic surveillance practices and leaked documents detailing the monitoring of US citizens to newspapers. This sparked great controversy on the government infringement of the privacy of its citizens. In 2015, President Obama and the US Senate passed the USA Freedom Act, which restored several provisions—in modified form—of the Patriot Act that had expired. For the first time, the law imposed limits on the collection of telecommunication data on US citizens by intelligence agencies.

CENSORING THE WEB

You can find almost anything on the web if you know where to look. Is this a good thing, or should there be some restrictions on what is available? Some of the material on the Internet is far more unpleasant than anything that is allowed in films, books, magazines, or television. Most countries have laws about what can be published in print or shown on screen. Should the web be any different?

Censorship is the examination of books, movies, letters, and digital content in order to remove things that are considered to be offensive, immoral, or harmful to society. It can be used to protect people from material that could damage or upset them. On the other hand, it can be used to restrict people's freedom by controlling their access to create or use information that they might use in undesirable ways. There is no worldwide censorship of the web, but most countries have laws that apply to online content within their borders. But producers of illegal material try to avoid prosecution by distributing across national boundaries, and international cooperation is required to stop such activity.

CENSORSHIP IN THE US

Different countries have their own purposes in censoring the web. In the West, our aims tend to be to protect children and other impressionable people; set limits on pornographic or violent material; block information that encourages crime; and prevent people from saying offensive things about other individuals or groups.

In the United States, child pornography is a federal crime. Any material that depicts minors (under the age of 18) in a sexually explicit way is illegal, so both downloading and uploading such content can be prosecuted. Authorities have been known to post fake child pornography websites in order to arrest people who visit them and try to find pictures or videos.

Along those lines, obscenity laws regulate materials or acts that are strongly offensive to general society's morality of the time. In the US, obscenity laws often come into conflict with issues of freedom of speech, which is protected by the First Amendment.

Cyberbullying on a social network is also illegal. Anyone who goes online and threatens to injure or kidnap someone or destroy their property can be fined or imprisoned for up to five years. This applies to threats and harassment that happen on e-mail, social media, or texting.

Scams to take money from people are crimes in the US. A common scam is a pyramid scheme where you may get an e-mail message with a subject about making money quickly by sending money to people on a list, adding your name to the list, and sending it on to a specified number of people.

FREEDOM VS. CENSORSHIP

Some people think that although it is right to protect children through censorship, adults should be free to view what they like. They say that adults should be able to make responsible choices and that we cannot protect them from everything. For example, we expect most people to drive cars safely, even though they could kill someone with their car. People who are against censorship believe in freedom of information—they feel that there should be no limits to what people can say, see, or hear in the media, Internet, or any other means of communication.

SIDEBAR

MUSIC THROUGH NAPSTER

Napster.com was a website that gathered users for sharing music. A member of Napster could upload music from a CD they had purchased, and another member could listen to it without buying a copy of the CD. Napster argued that this was, in theory, legal. The company compared their service to someone who invites friends to her house to listen to a new CD. The problem was that the Napster website was open to anyone, so effectively the whole world could share music without buying it. The music industry objected to this and took Napster to court. They claimed that Napster was making their copyrighted music available illegally. Although Napster may have had a case in defense, they ran out of money fighting the court action and closed down.

copyright

p2p

crime

TORRENT

illegal   piracy

download

Other people think that we should all be protected from damaging material. They believe that if we see too much violence, we may become hardened to it and accept or carry it out in the real world more readily. They also argue that graphic sex or violence in films, websites, or computer games can be so upsetting that it causes us emotional or psychological damage. So they believe we should ban it in the same way that we ban dangerous drugs that cause physical harm.

In 1997, a new law called the Communications Decency Act was drawn up, aiming to restrict pornography and other explicit material, but it was ruled illegal by the US Supreme Court because it would restrict what could be published on websites and violate the US Constitution's First Amendment right to the freedom of speech and the press.

Countries such as Iran ban or limit Internet access because they fear their way of life will change if people are influenced by Western ideas.

Even pages that do not appear to intend harm to others can be damaging if they are seen by impressionable people. Some sites might set an example that seems unacceptable to the rest of society—promoting the positive effects of drugs, for instance. Some people might think these sites should be censored, but others may feel this violates their personal freedom.

COMPLEXITIES OF PROTECTION

Many believe some sites should be censored if they give people details on how to hurt one another—ones that explain how to make weapons, kill, or torture people, for example. Information like this is available in some books, but these are more difficult to get hold of. The web makes such information available to everyone.

Rating systems are now being developed to help people restrict which websites they can see on their own computers. Parents can protect their children—or themselves—by installing filtering programs on their web browsers or using "safe search" mode on their search engines. Some filters work by allowing only suitably rated pages to be displayed—but as many sites are not rated, this can be overly restrictive. Other filters try to judge what is in a page and decide whether it can or cannot be seen—but they are not always reliable because they may not pick up all unpleasant material. Many use the Internet in public places such as libraries and schools. In such locations, filters are generally used, but this is not always the case with places such as Internet cafes of hotels.

Children and other impressionable people are exposed to many risks if they use the Internet in an unprotected environment. They may be lured into an online chat and perhaps a meeting with someone who seems friendly but in fact intends harm—it is easy to be anonymous on the Internet or to pretend to be someone you are not. They might receive unpleasant spam e-mail, be drawn into online gambling they cannot afford, or be recruited by discriminatory groups.

Some websites may be intended to cause problems for particular individuals. Information such as the release dates of prisoners, along with their criminal records, can be put on a website for anyone to see. There are sex-offender registries in every state that identify people convicted as sexual perpetrators, including where they live. These may warn people that they could be at risk when criminals are freed or if a sex offender lives in the neighborhood—or it could be intended to expose them to harassment.

Because of the way the Internet works, it is very difficult to make anyone responsible for what happens there. At the moment, most who feel they have been damaged by what they have seen or done online is on their own—it is up to individuals to avoid looking at harmful material. But many Internet users know little about the dangers or how to avoid them. Is this fair? Perhaps we should expect the people who make money from selling us computers, software, and Internet connections to do more to protect people. Or is it more realistic to accept that we should all learn to take responsibility for our own well-being online?

LIMITED ACCESS

There are some countries in which Internet use is restricted by the government. People either are not afforded the equipment to access the Internet, or they can only look at a restricted range of websites. Does a country have the right to impose these rules?

Information and multimedia that is posted on the Internet is dominated by the West and particularly by the US. Many countries do not share Western views, including religious, cultural, and political ideas. Some of the material available on the web is also against the law in many places. For instance, a website on brewing beer would be illegal in countries where alcohol is not allowed. For these reasons, other nations may want to keep Western websites from its people.

Much of our lifestyle is bound up with religious ideas—and they are not shared by everyone in the world. Some of the images and practices that are part of everyday life, such as how people dress, in the West may be offensive to people with different traditions and beliefs. Some countries want to block Western sites and other Internet services to protect their people from material that they consider spiritually or morally damaging.

In Myanmar (previously Burma), authorities filter e-mail and block access to sites that expose human rights violations in the country or disagree with the government. In North Korea, all websites are under government control, and only four percent of the population has Internet access. The governments of other countries such as Cuba, Saudi Arabia, and Iran restrict websites and filter content to promote state goals. China has the most rigid censorship program in the world, where the government filters searches, block sites, and deletes content that it does not approve of. It even reroutes search terms on Taiwan independence or the Tiananmen Square massacre to pages favorable to the Communist Party.

In some countries, access to Western news sites or webpages of human rights organizations is banned. The Chinese government has expressed disagreement with the way US journalists interpret the news. After the terrorist attacks on the US in September, 2001, the Chinese people wanted more detailed information. The government eased restrictions on the web but continued to block many major US news sites. They have also maintained a ban on human rights sites—such as www.amnesty.org—which they feel will encourage their people to question the way they are treated.

TEXT-DEPENDENT QUESTIONS

1. What are the possible civil and criminal penalties for illegally copying and distributing music or movies online?

2. Name four pieces of information identity thieves may look to steal from you.

3. What is one method authorities have used to arrest criminals who violate child pornography laws?

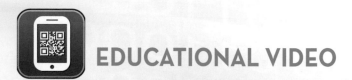 **EDUCATIONAL VIDEO**

Scan here to watch a video on cyberbullying.

RESEARCH PROJECT

Using the Internet or your school library, research the topic of First Amendment rights and the Internet, and answer the following question: "Should all content be free to view and post on the Internet?"

Some contend that anything should be allowed on the Internet because the First Amendment protects the freedom of speech and the press. People should be able to express themselves, and everyone should be able to watch, read, or listen to whatever they want because they assume responsibility for their actions.

Others argue that a healthy and balanced society needs Internet restrictions. Pornography objectifies women and is essentially a digital form of prostitution—payment for sexual gratification. Websites that can be used for human trafficking or to teach ways to hurt people should absolutely be banned. There is a great deal of content that is harmful to both children and adults, and just as there are laws against hateful propaganda, there should be laws that govern online content.

Write a two-page report, using data you have found in your research to support your conclusion, and present it to your class.

WORDS TO UNDERSTAND

ethics—an area of study that deals with ideas about what is good and bad behavior: a branch of philosophy dealing with what is morally right or wrong

pandemic—an outbreak of a disease that occurs over a wide geographic area and affects an exceptionally high proportion of the population

philosopher—a person who studies ideas about knowledge, truth, the nature and meaning of life, etc.

unbiased—not having or showing an unfair tendency to believe that some people, ideas, etc., are better than others; not biased

vested interest—a personal or private reason for wanting something to be done or to happen

CHAPTER 5

MOVING TOWARD THE FUTURE

DIGITAL TECHNOLOGY IMPROVES EFFICIENCY in many areas of life. We can learn about a variety of topics by typing on a search engine rather than having to find experts and consult them. We can order products with one click, and goods can appear at our doorstep within a day or two, often at a cheaper price than what we can find by going to a store. A movie can be played at home in high definition with surround-sound effects. With all of this technology, how are we using the extra time and energy the Digital Age affords us? How will society be shaped as we move forward?

Many teens have been told at some point to stop playing online games and do something more valuable with their time. Are we in fact better off with digital technologies, or do we just have more time to squander? Does it really matter if we spend a lot of time online?

Some people believe that parents should be responsible for monitoring what their children see on the Web. Others feel that laws should be passed that would prevent the need for parental oversight.

INCREASES IN GAMING

According to a 2014 Nielsen 360 Gaming Report, players aged 13 and up spend more than 6 hours a week playing games on all platforms, a 12 percent increase from 5.6 hours in 2012.

 **SIDEBAR**

VIDEO GAME RATINGS

As there are ratings for what types of audiences are appropriate for various movies, there are also ratings for video games. The Entertainment Software Rating Board (ESRB) ratings provide guidance about video games and apps so that consumers, especially parents, can make informed choices about what is suitable to play. The ratings have three parts:

- Rating categories suggest age appropriateness: early childhood, everyone, everyone 10+, teen, mature 17+, and adults only 18+.
- Content descriptors indicate which content may have triggered a particular rating and/or may be of concern (e.g., "Comic Mischief," "Mild Lyrics").
- Interactive elements inform about users' ability to interact, the sharing of users' location with others, if personal information may be shared with third parties, if in-app purchases of digital goods are completed, and/or if unrestricted Internet access is provided.

Mobile and tablet gaming accounted for 19 percent of time spent gaming, up from 9 percent in 2011. Tablet play rose the most overall, accounting for 9 percent of all weekly game time, more than twice the 4 percent it comprised in 2012. Smartphone time rose slightly to 10 percent, up 1 percent from 2012.

Dedicated video game players who own console systems are picking up tablets and smartphones too, with 50 percent of them saying they play a mobile device, up from 46 percent in 2012 and 35 percent in 2011. Video games on consoles such as the PlayStation 3, Xbox 360, and Wii accounted for the most gaming time (34 percent) despite a 3 percent drop from 2012. New systems such as the PS4, Xbox One, and Wii U made up 4 percent of game time. Overall, nearly two-thirds of the population (64 percent) play video games on some device, a figure that has remained stable since 2010.

A report from The NPD Group showed the average time spent playing mobile games in 2014 increased by 57 percent compared to 2012. People spent about 3 hours every day playing games on their iPhones, Android devices, and tablets. In 2012, that figure was

The popular "augmented reality" smartphone game Pokemon GO shows a Pokemon encounter on a trail in the forest. The character appears on the phone in the area where the user is. Pokemon GO was released in July 2016.

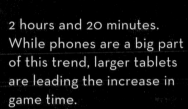

2 hours and 20 minutes. While phones are a big part of this trend, larger tablets are leading the increase in game time.

The NPD notes that not only do people spend more time playing games on tablets, but these gamers are also more likely to spend money. Indeed, mobile gaming has grown into a $25 billion market. Youth between the ages of 2 and 12 spend the most time gaming on mobile devices. This group played five different games on average and were second only to gamers aged 25 to 44 in spending money on new games and in-app purchases in 2014.

SOCIAL MEDIA TRENDS

Social platforms have become the new leaders in the digital media industry, expanding from digital communication networks to full-fledged media distribution channels and entertainment centers. In 2016, comScore reported that nearly 20 percent of total time spent online in the US across both desktop and mobile devices is on social platforms. Facebook alone, makes up a whopping 14 percent of total time spent online.

A 2015 study from Informate Mobile Intelligence revealed people in the US check their Facebook, Twitter, and other social media accounts 17 times a day. But people in the US are not even the most dependent on these networks when compared to those in

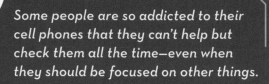

Some people are so addicted to their cell phones that they can't help but check them all the time—even when they should be focused on other things.

other countries—in fact, smartphone users in Thailand, Argentina, Malaysia, Qatar, Mexico, and South Africa checked social networking apps at least 40 times a day. The majority of these compulsive social media checkers are not teens but adults, with the highest usage observed in those between the ages of 25 and 54.

SMARTPHONE ADDICTION

The research from Informate Mobile Intelligence found that in 2015, while the US did not lead global markets in amount of time spent on social media networks, it was far and away the highest consumer of monthly data, spending the most time on their cell phones at an astounding 4.7 hours per day. Considering that the average person in the US is awake for just over 15 hours a day, this means that we spend approximately one-third of our waking hours on our phones. Some of that time may be doing work, but, as the above studies show, significant amounts are on social media and online games.

According to a survey by AT&T and the Center for Internet and Technology Addiction, 61 percent of people in the US sleep with their phones and 53 percent get upset to different degrees if they do not have their phones with them. This phone uneasiness in fact has a term: "nomophobia" is the fear of being without one's smartphone, and it affects 40 percent of the US population.

Research into frequent digital use has come up with varied results. Some studies have found that, because using the Internet is a solitary activity, it can damage social skills. People who spend long periods of time alone may find it harder to relate to others. They might find conversation more difficult or feel shy in public. In this way, the isolation resulting from digital devices could be damaging to society. The web may also draw people away from other activities, such as sports, which some people would argue are more beneficial.

Other studies suggest that in other ways, regular digital use can be positive. People may become technology savvy with skills in programming or other computer technologies. Likewise, games can improve skills such as reflexes, logic, and visual awareness.

QUALITY AND CONTENT

Some material on the web is of very high quality. It can be educational, culturally diverse, and enjoyable at the same time. The web can, for instance, bring classical music, art exhibitions, or the chance to learn a foreign language to people who may otherwise miss out on such opportunities. It can be a good source of entertainment and accurate, useful, information.

But there is also a lot of poor quality material on the Internet—such as games that do not develop any useful skills and unsavory material with graphic violence or gross sexual content. People worry that this content may encourage violence or unhealthy sexuality in the real world, if not psychological damage.

Freedom of speech can lead to better understanding between people. But freedom of speech on the Internet can also help people to spread racial prejudice or abuse specific groups of people.

Earlier in the book, we discussed countries that limit Internet access for political and religious reasons. Places like this may also ban websites in the hope of preserving national culture and tradition. People in some nations think that the ready availability of Western culture—especially from the US—has led to the decline in other ways of life. For example, some people in developing countries may neglect local traditions in favor of aspects of Western culture that they see on television and the web. This could be anything from cartoons to pop music or online games. If a consumerist mentality also grows in areas where it previously did not exist, people may become resentful if they want goods that are not available to them.

In each country, there is a need for guidance on how to navigate the Digital Age. What Internet material should be allowed, and who should determine the parameters? If digital addiction—to games, social media, or phones in general—continues to increase, it may be considered a social ill or even a type of *pandemic*, a disease that spreads very quickly and affects many people over a wide area. What programs or policies might be used to promote a healthier lifestyle, perhaps with more outdoor activity or live human interaction?

DEVELOPING A CODE OF ETHICS

The realm of *ethics*—dealing with right and wrong choices—may need to expand beyond gun laws or animal rights now that we are in a new era. Whenever we make a decision, we take into account a variety of factors, many of which are ethical issues. In some

Many remote places have no laws regarding the Internet. One of these places could be used to host a website that would be illegal in the United States or other countries with restrictive laws.

cases, many people agree, leading to ethical issues being built into laws. For example, most people agree that we should not kill or take someone else's property, so murder and theft are generally illegal throughout the world. But there is disagreement over other ethical questions. Many vegetarians believe it is wrong to kill animals to eat, for instance, but other people do not have a problem with this. In some cases, there are cultural, religious, or regional differences that influence people's moral stances. In the West, most people believe we should be allowed to marry who we wish, but in many other countries, arranged marriages between people who have never met are common and even seen as the best system for couples.

Over time, countries develop systems of what they believe is right and wrong. A code of ethics is not thought up by an individual at one stroke, but they evolve over time with learning and experience by whole populations. Our ideas of morality generally help societies to grow in positive ways, but where there is disagreement, there may be debate or conflict.

ETHICS FOR THE DIGITAL AGE

Developing a code of ethics in a new field is complicated and often difficult, but we must work to create one if we seek to integrate digital technologies into society in a healthy manner. Many ethical codes are closely tied to religious beliefs. In countries such as the US, people are allowed to follow any religion they wish, and the law tries to support them in practicing their faith. In other places, there is one religion that is approved by the state, and all other faiths are banned. Presumably, these countries would want the Internet to be governed according to their religious and ethical codes.

It is very difficult for people to make *unbiased* decisions—not influenced by their own feelings, opinions, or interests. In some areas, we may think we are not biased, as everyone we know would make the same choice. But we may be showing a national or cultural bias. Everyone you know may agree that boys and girls have an equal right to education, but this is not held to be true everywhere.

Just as there are current arguments regarding topics such as genetic engineering and abortion, countries may disagree about what should and should not be allowed on the Internet. Still, legal restrictions for each country and for the world are necessary because as the digital world continues to develop, not all technology will be used for good purposes—there are criminals in every field. They may use online resources for financial or military objectives, from identity theft to cyberterrorism. It is important to have guidelines for what is right and wrong as well as how to enforce them, but who should develop those policies?

ETHICS COMMITTEES

We have seen throughout this book how the Digital Age influences many different aspects of our lives—wealth distribution, economic industries, social interaction, education, and so on. There are also questions of right and wrong in each of these sectors. Who is monitoring the development of digital hardware and software and the risks posed to us by new advances?

Ethics committees are groups of people who meet to discuss the work carried out by scientists in research institutions and hospitals. Some of the members are subject experts, and some are *philosophers* with an interest in ethics or morals. Philosophers study ideas about knowledge, truth, and the meaning of life. They may think about issues such as what is right and wrong, how we develop a code of ethics, and the good of society versus the good of the individual.

Beyond debating amongst themselves, ethics committees will likely have to dialogue with people who have expertise other arenas, such as computer programming, economics, or politics. An ethics committee tries to represent the views of everyone who will have an interest in an issue as it makes decisions about what is right and wrong—or what should be allowed and what should not. With a full team assembled, they discuss individual cases as well as more abstract issues.

An ethics committee in a hospital might review the case of an individual patient, or it might be appointed by the government to investigate if research into a particular area should be permitted. In digital technology, a committee may study the drawbacks of allowing government surveillance of people's online use against the benefits of increased security. It may explore the damage of online pornography versus the rights of the First Amendment. Each country may draw up its own laws, and in some areas of research, these can differ considerably.

Many of the people working in controversial fields such as digital content have a *vested interest*—they may be trying to make money or further their own careers. But in a specialized area, these people, who may be biased, are the ones who often know most about the issues. How they explain things can make a huge difference to society because our opinions may depend on the information they supply. Thus, it is beneficial if general citizens are learning themselves about issues at hand.

We need to be sure we are basing our views on relevant facts and not on

biased arguments. The more informed we are about issues in the Digital Age, the more capable we will be in creating balanced guidelines for the areas affected by its technologies. Whether it is in reorganizing the labor force after AI programs take over more and more human jobs or finding productive uses of time in an era of newfound efficiency, the future will be best served by knowledgeable individuals who work together for society.

TEXT-DEPENDENT QUESTIONS

1. How much time does the average person in the US spend on their cell phone? What fraction of their waking hours does that make up?

2. What are two types of people that may be members of an ethics committee?

 **EDUCATIONAL VIDEO**

Scan here to watch a video on an example of ethics in the Digital Age.

RESEARCH PROJECT

Using the Internet or your school library, research the topic of social media and relationships, and answer the following question: "Does social media increase healthy relationships between people?"

Some believe that social media makes relationships between people less healthy because they are only exchanging brief messages or reading status updates about one another. People become saturated with shallow interactions and become unaccustomed to spending extended time face-to-face, where there is more authenticity, depth, and creativity.

Others maintain that social media leads to healthier relationships because people maintain contact with each other more frequently, know what is happening in each other's lives, and may meet more people through networking sites. This is simply the way relationships have evolved in the Digital Age.

Write a two-page report, using data you have found in your research to support your conclusion, and present it to your class.

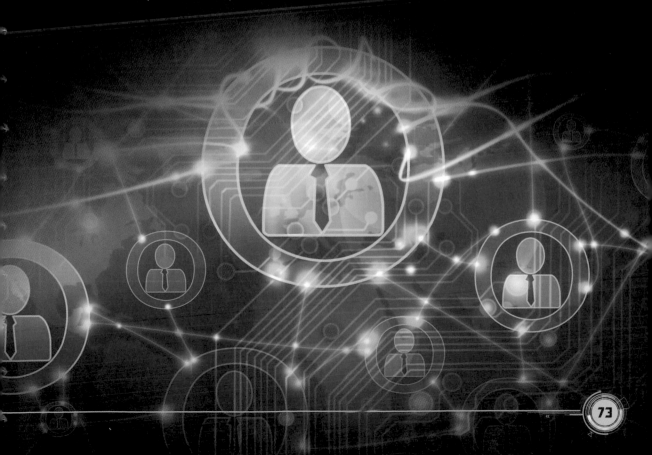

SERIES GLOSSARY OF KEY TERMS

anomaly—something that differs from the expectations generated by an established scientific idea. Anomalous observations may inspire scientists to reconsider, modify, or come up with alternatives to an accepted theory or hypothesis.

evidence—test results and/or observations that may either help support or help refute a scientific idea. In general, raw data are considered evidence only once they have been interpreted in a way that reflects on the accuracy of a scientific idea.

experiment—a scientific test that involves manipulating some factor or factors in a system in order to see how those changes affect the outcome or behavior of the system.

hypothesis—a proposed explanation for a fairly narrow set of phenomena, usually based on prior experience, scientific background knowledge, preliminary observations, and logic.

natural world—all the components of the physical universe, as well as the natural forces at work on those things.

objective—to consider and represent facts without being influenced by biases, opinions, or emotions. Scientists strive to be objective, not subjective, in their reasoning about scientific issues.

observe—to note, record, or attend to a result, occurrence, or phenomenon.

science—knowledge of the natural world, as well as the process through which that knowledge is built through testing ideas with evidence gathered from the natural world.

subjective—referring to something that is influenced by biases, opinions, and/or emotions. Scientists strive to be objective, not subjective, in their reasoning about scientific issues.

test—an observation or experiment that could provide evidence regarding the accuracy of a scientific idea. Testing involves figuring out what one would expect to observe if an idea were correct and comparing that expectation to what one actually observes.

theory—a broad, natural explanation for a wide range of phenomena in science. Theories are concise, coherent, systematic, predictive, and broadly applicable, often integrating and generalizing many hypotheses. Theories accepted by the scientific community are generally strongly supported by many different lines of evidence. However, theories may be modified or overturned as new evidence is discovered.

FURTHER READING

Doan, Andrew P., Brooke Strickland, and Douglas Gentile. *Hooked on Games: The Lure and Cost of Video Game and Internet Addiction.* Coralville, Iowa: FEP International, 2012.

Hinduja, Sameer, and Justin W. Patchin. *Bullying Beyond the Schoolyard: Preventing and Responding to Cyberbullying.* Thousand Oaks, Calif.: Corwin, 2015.

Kelly, John E. III. *Smart Machines: IBM's Watson and the Era of Cognitive Computing.* New York: Columbia University Press, 2013.

Steiner-Adair, Catherine, and Teresa H. Barker. *The Big Disconnect: Protecting Childhood and Family Relationships in the Digital Age.* New York: Harper Paperbacks, 2014.

Stuckey, Rachel. *Digital Dangers.* New York: Crabtree Publishing Company, 2015.

Turkle, Sherry. *Reclaiming Conversation: The Power of Talk in a Digital Age.* New York:

INTERNET RESOURCES

https://www.stopbullying.gov/cyberbullying/ This website addresses all types of bullying, including cyberbullying, which happens when kids bully each other through electronic technology. Find out why cyberbullying is different from traditional bullying, what you can do to prevent it, and how you can report it when it happens.

http://www.netsmartz.org/Teens NetSmartz Workshop is an interactive, educational program of the National Center for Missing & Exploited Children (NCMEC) that provides age-appropriate resources to teach children how to be safer on- and offline. The program is designed for children ages 5-17, with videos, games, activity cards, and presentations, to entertain while it educates. It teaches how to recognize potential Internet risks, prevent yourself from being exploited, and report victimization to a trusted adult.

http://www.digitaltrends.com/ Digital Trends helps readers easily understand how technology affects the way they live. It offers the latest news, videos, and product reviews in digital technology.

https://www.esrb.org/ The Entertainment Software Rating Board (ESRB) assigns age and content ratings for video games and mobile apps, enforces advertising and marketing guidelines for the video game industry, and helps companies implement responsible online and mobile privacy practices.

http://aitopics.org/ AITopics is a collection of information about the research, people, and applications of artificial intelligence. Its mission is to educate and inspire through a wide variety of organized resources gathered from across the web, including articles, videos, podcasts, and book references.

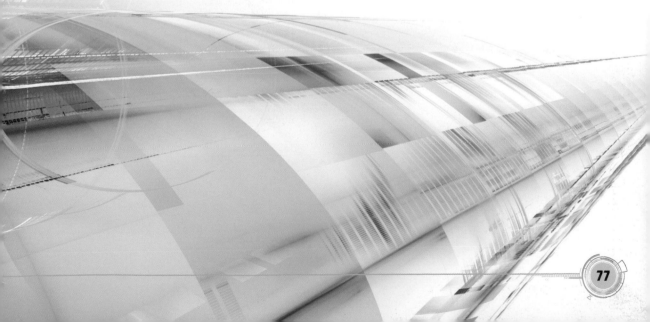

INDEX

Numbers in **bold italics** refer to captions.

ABOUT THE AUTHOR

Beatrice Kavanaugh is a graduate of Bryn Mawr College. A former newspaper writer and editor, she currently works as a freelance writer. She also wrote the book *Medical Discoveries* in this series.

PUBLISHER'S NOTE

The websites that are cited in this book were active at the time of publication. The publisher is not responsible for websites that have changed their address or discontinued operation since the date of publication. The publisher reviews and updates the websites each time this book is reprinted.

PHOTO CREDITS